I Am Not a PAPER ROLL!

by Emily Kington

HUNGRY TOMATO™

MINNEAPOLIS

Contents

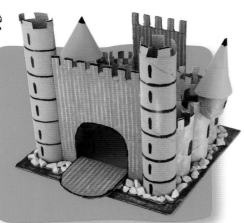
You will need a grown-up to help you make these fantastic models.

Ready to Have Fun?

Recycling unwanted things into art is really fun, and it doesn't cost a fortune—all the main materials in this book were going to be thrown away!

Rescue paper rolls from your recycling bin and get crafty. You will soon have your very own art collection.

See page 24 for more information about materials.

You will need...

Paper rolls
Masking tape
Craft glue
Pipe cleaners
Egg carton
Buttons or beads
Plastic eyes
String
Cotton swabs

Cardboard
Small stick
Paper
Tissue paper
Paper plate
Paintbrush
Acrylic paint
Pen
Markers
Hole punch

Spooky Friends

This spooky centerpiece would be perfect if you ever throw a Halloween party!

You will need...

Cardboard	Small stick
Paper rolls	Pen
Pipe cleaner	Masking tape
String	Acrylic paint
Egg carton	Paintbrush
Tissue paper	Craft glue
Paper	Marker
Paper clay	(optional)

Spooky Friends

1 **Use** one paper roll for the witch. Paint the body and head.

Trim and paint strands of string orange. Glue on to make hair.

Then paint the mouth and teeth!

2 **Trim** a paper roll to make a small owl.

Fold in the top to make the owl's ears. Color or paint the owl.

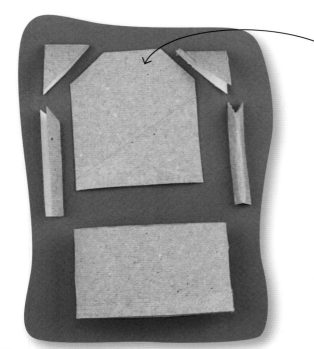

3 **Flatten** a paper roll and trim into this shape. Use the cut off pieces for the cat's ears.

To make a curly tail, wind a pipe cleaner around a pen. Attach it with masking tape.

5 Make some spooky accessories:

Make a cauldron from an egg carton. Add string for a handle.

Build a fire using string. Paint it black and red.

Make a broomstick by taping together a small stick and some string.

Use small pieces of paper clay to make eyes.

4 Draw around a round object and cut out the circle.

Fold it in half and draw a line to the center. Then cut along the line.

Fold into a cone shape and glue into place. Bend to make an edge, cut the rim, and paint it black.

6 Paint a cardboard base and place all three of the spooky friends onto it.

Paint the cat and glue on the paper clay eyes and string whiskers.

Fill the cauldron with tissue paper.

Zoo Animals

You can make all sorts of animals using paper rolls. These two are real winners!

You will need...

Giraffe
Paper rolls
Cotton swabs
Masking tape
Craft glue
String
Beads
Pipe cleaner
Acrylic paint
Paintbrush

Zebra
Paper rolls
Pipe cleaner
String
Masking tape
Craft glue
Plastic eyes
Acrylic paint
Paintbrush

Recycled animal friends, perfect together!

9

Zoo Animals
Giraffe

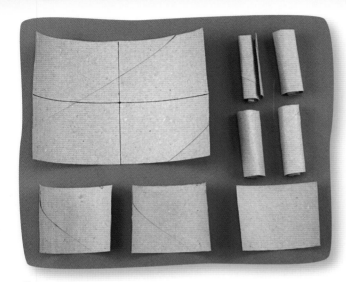

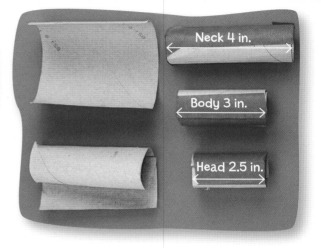

Neck 4 in.

Body 3 in.

Head 2.5 in.

1 **Flatten** a paper roll. Cut down one side lengthwise and open it up. Divide into four equal pieces and roll them up to form the legs. Stick together with masking tape.

2 **Cut** three more paper rolls lengthwise and use them to make the neck, head, and body.

Trim to the lengths above and roll into shape. Stick together with masking tape.

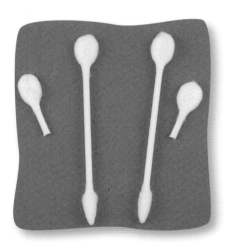

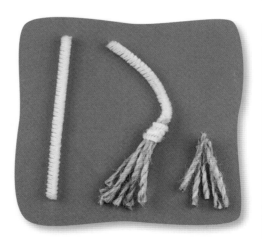

3 **Trim** two cotton swabs and paint them.

4 **Make a tail** using a pipe cleaner and string.

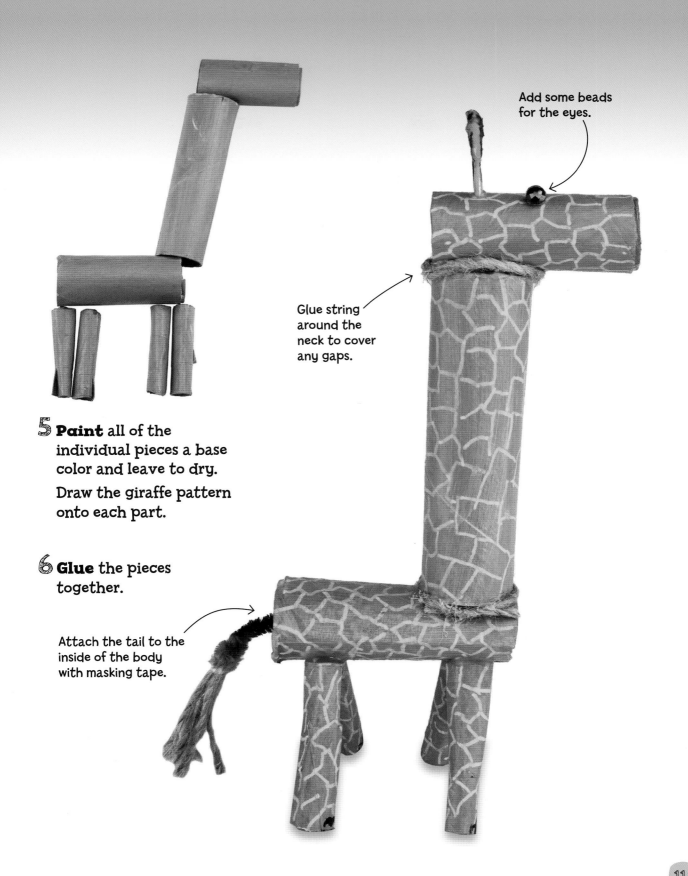

Add some beads for the eyes.

Glue string around the neck to cover any gaps.

5 **Paint** all of the individual pieces a base color and leave to dry.

Draw the giraffe pattern onto each part.

6 **Glue** the pieces together.

Attach the tail to the inside of the body with masking tape.

Zoo Animals Zebra

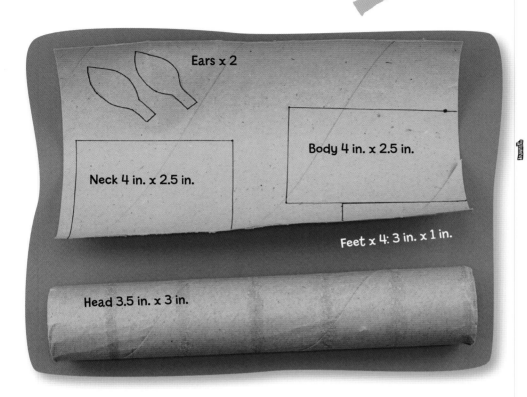

Ears x 2

Neck 4 in. x 2.5 in.

Body 4 in. x 2.5 in.

Feet x 4: 3 in. x 1 in.

Head 3.5 in. x 3 in.

1 Cut two large paper rolls lengthwise and open them up. Use them to make the body parts.

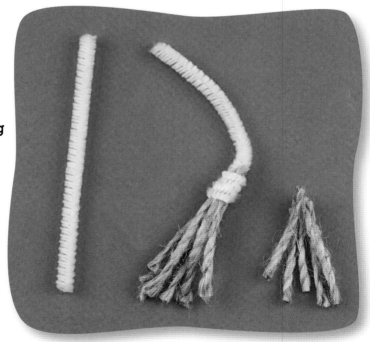

2 Make a tail using string and a pipe cleaner.

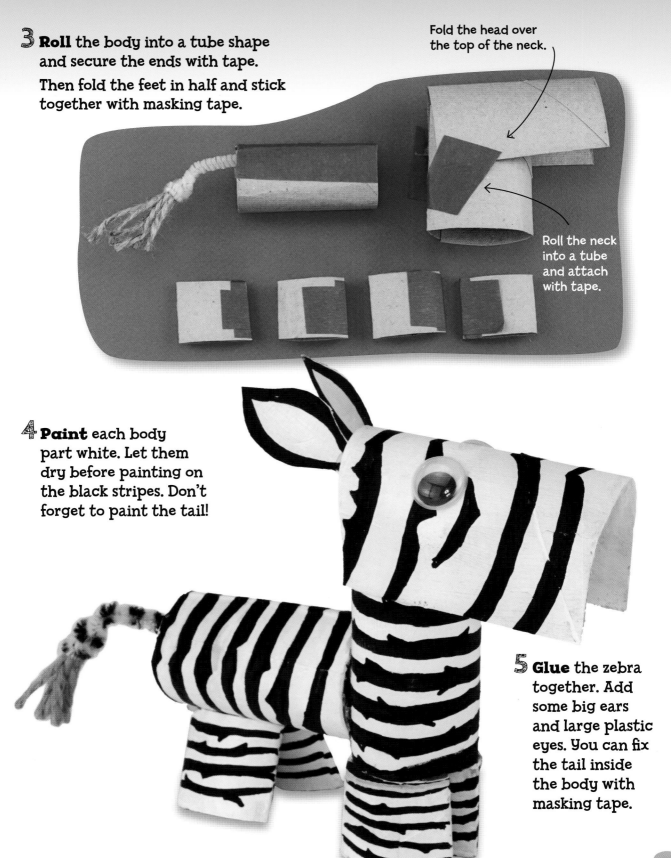

3 Roll the body into a tube shape and secure the ends with tape.

Then fold the feet in half and stick together with masking tape.

Fold the head over the top of the neck.

Roll the neck into a tube and attach with tape.

4 Paint each body part white. Let them dry before painting on the black stripes. Don't forget to paint the tail!

5 Glue the zebra together. Add some big ears and large plastic eyes. You can fix the tail inside the body with masking tape.

13

Hungry Frog

Hold your frog, flip up the fly, and be ready to catch it!

You will need...

- Paper rolls
- String
- Craft glue
- Paper
- Marker
- Hole punch
- Acrylic paint
- Paintbrush
- Masking tape (optional)

Catch the fly in the frog's mouth!

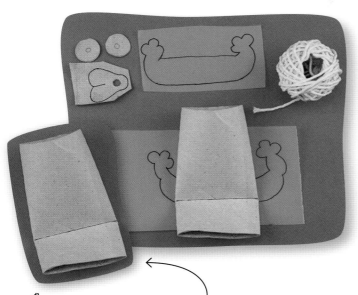

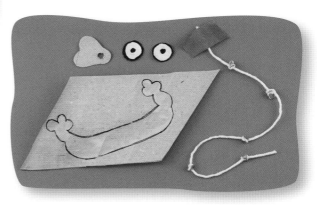

2

Cut another paper roll lengthwise and flatten it.

Glue on the back and front legs and cut them out.

Draw some big eyes and a fly. Cut them out. Use a hole punch to make a hole in the fly.

Cut a length of string and make a few knots.

1

Fold the bottom portion of a paper roll like this.

Make a template on paper of the four legs and cut them out.

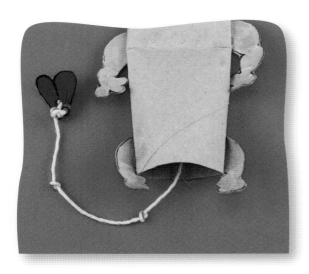

3

Glue the front and back legs to the paper roll.

Thread the fly onto the string. Make a big knot at the end so he doesn't escape!

Attach the string with masking tape or glue.

4

Paint the inside red and the outside bright green.

Glue on the eyes.

Crafty Caterpillar

This caterpillar is really useful. He can carry lots of helpful tools for all of your art projects.

You will need...

Paper rolls
Pipe cleaner
Egg carton
Paper clay
Craft glue
Paper plate
String
Pen
Acrylic paint
Paintbrush
Markers (optional)

This really is a crafty caterpillar!

Crafty Caterpillar

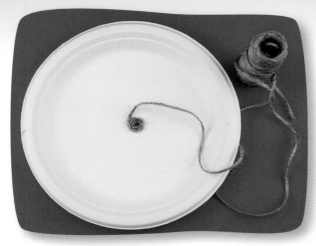

1 **Decorate** the center of your plate with a wheel of string. Wind the string around and glue as you go! Decorate the edges with paints or markers.

2 **Make** the caterpillar antennae by winding a pipe cleaner around a pen.

Cut out one of the egg carton cups to make the head.

Make some eyes out of paper clay.

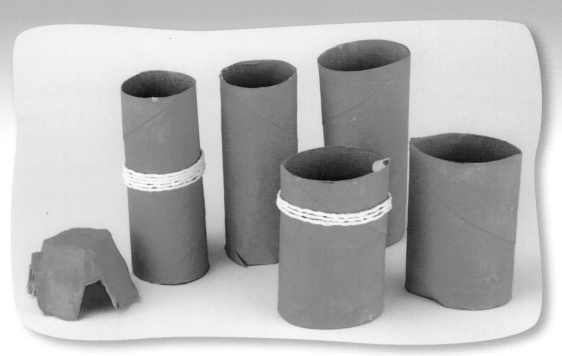

3 **Paint** the head and paper rolls and leave to dry.
Add some string for decoration!

4 **Assemble** the caterpillar
and glue to the plate.

Add a little glue to
the string so the
paper rolls stick
to each other.

Add your own
decoration—leaves,
buttons, or beads.

Castle

You can make this castle any size you like as long as you have saved enough paper rolls from the recycling bin!

A castle fit for a king and a princess or two . . . and ready for battle!

You will need...

Paper rolls
Cardboard
Colored paper
Gravel
Chalk
Craft glue
Acrylic paint
Paintbrush
Markers

Castle

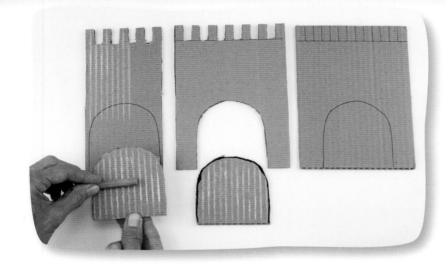

1 **Draw** these shapes onto cardboard to make the entrances to the castle.

Cut out the entrance door and the top as shown.

Drag the side of a piece of chalk down each piece of the cardboard.

To make a castle turret, cut a slit and attach to another paper roll.

2 Use small and large paper rolls for the castle walls and towers. Paint them and draw on windows and arrow slits.

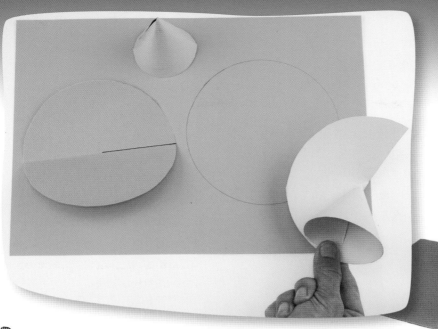

4 **Assemble** your castle on a cardboard base. Choose where you want to put the different pieces.

Leave room for a moat.

3 **Use** colored paper to make roofs for the turrets. First, draw around a round object and cut out a circle.

Draw a line to the center, then cut along the line.

Fold into a cone shape and glue into place.

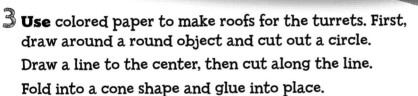

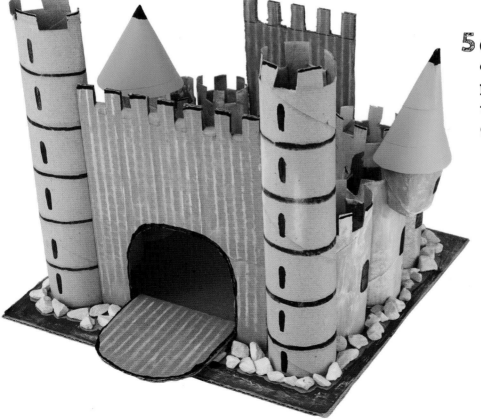

5 **Glue** all of the pieces onto the base.

Paint a moat all around the castle and glue gravel around the base.

Useful Items

Paper clay is great for fine detail and has been used to make some of the eyes.

It's a good thing to add to your craft box. It can be purchased cheaply from craft stores and online.

A little goes a long way. It just needs to air-dry before painting.

It's fun to use, but you can also use plastic eyes from craft stores or just paint eyes onto your projects.

3 water jars for cleaning brushes while painting.

Scissors

Ruler

Picture Credits

(abbreviations: t = top; b = bottom; m = middle; l = left; r = right; bg = background)

Shutterstock:
AKIllustration 4tl, 5tr; archivector 14bl; Baurz1973 14bg; Evgeniya Mokeeva 21mr; FARBAI 16bl; GraphicsRF 16bg; Juliann 20bg; Makyzz 4bg; Malika Keehl 8bg; Marina Linchevska 10bl.

Hungry Tomato®
A division of Lerner Publishing Group, Inc.
241 First Avenue North
Minneapolis, MN 55401 USA

For reading levels and more information, look up this title at www.lernerbooks.com.

Main body text set in Billy Serif Regular.

Library of Congress Cataloging-in-Publication Data

Names: Kington, Emily, 1961- author.
Title: I am not a paper roll! / Emily Kington.
Description: Minneapolis : Hungry Tomato, [2018] | Series: Ready-made recycling | Audience: Age 6-9. | Audience: K to Grade 3.
Identifiers: LCCN 2018054441 (print) | LCCN 2018055180 (ebook) | ISBN 9781541555204 (eb pdf) | ISBN 9781541555198 (lb : alk. paper)
Subjects: LCSH: Cardboard tube craft—Juvenile literature.
Classification: LCC TT870 (ebook) | LCC TT870 .K5283 2018 (print) | DDC 745.592—dc23

LC record available at https://lccn.loc.gov/2018054441

Manufactured in the United States of America
1-45927-42821-1/10/2019